Book of Disquiet:
Dispatches From the Disability Frontlines

Carter Hammett

These articles previously appeared in *Communiqué* and *Abilities* magazines

Editor: Taru Virkamaki
Proofreading: Sue Stanley
Cover Design and Photography: Carter Hammett

Wordgarden Press
Toronto, Ontario (Canada)
www.wordgarden.ca

Printed and bound in Canada
ISBN: 978-0-9737264-2-8

ACKNOWLEDGEMENTS

First and foremost, I'd like to acknowledge and thank the terrific people, past and present that I've had the good fortune to work with at the Learning Disabilities Association of Ontario (www.ldao.ca), including Diane Wagner, Karen Quinn and Lawrence Barns. Working together on *Communiqué* and documenting the evolution of learning disabilities information continues to be both a pleasure and a privilege, which I hope continues for a long time to come.

I'd also like to thank my former editors at *Abilities Magazine* (www.abilities.ca) Jaclyn Law, Lisa Bendall and Jennifer Rivkin for their insights and guidance as we tortured my rambling pieces into submission and reader-worthiness.

There are friends, some new, many old, that I remain eternally grateful to and inspired by and they include Dave Dickson, Nigel Pickup, Ross MacDonald, Darrel Kane Gladue, Dennis Bowman, Jamie Proctor, John Chew, Thomas Chau, Ken and Maria Seaton, Kate Kelner, Isabella Carrera, Colette Legault, Sue Stanley, Zoë Kessler, Archna Kurichh, Chrystalla Chew, Wendy Symes and Dave Leaf and not least, Taru Virkamaki. Thank you all for your amazing support and friendship!

Sue Stanley had the manuscript passed on to her for proofreading and her sharp eyes quickly identified details that slipped through the cracks. Any errors that remain are mine alone. I'd especially like to thank my friend and editor Taru Virkamaki who tackled this project with an unrivalled zest and good natured ribbing throughout the entire process. Working together has been simply, a blast!

And finally, I'd like to take a moment and acknowledge all the people who consented to be interviewed for the pieces contained in this little book. I am moved and honoured to have spent time, however brief with you, and to be allowed a glimpse into the gifts you give the world. I hope the essays gathered here do justice to the work you do. You're the reason this book exists.

By the same author:

Conscious Competence: A Skills Training Program
for Mentoring Persons with Learning Disabilities (2006)

Benchmarking: A Guide to Hiring and Managing
Persons with Learning Disabilities (co-author, 2005)

Community Connections: A Directory of Community
and Social Services in York Region (Editor, 2001)

In memory of

Stephen Jones,
Sue Dupuis
Mitchell Kelner
and
Bob Antosik

Gone too soon

Book of Disquiet

TABLE OF CONTENTS

Introduction: On Reading Again

Back in 2011 I finally had the opportunity to meet one of my Learning

Disability (LD) heroes, Rick Lavoie. There was just one little problem--the creator of the famous F.A.T. City workshops and author of *It's So Much Work to Be Your Friend* among other influential works, had been living in my Blackberry for about six months.

Now before you start thinking that we're best friends and were carrying on a jovial correspondence, let me clarify something. I had been receiving *daily* emails from the one-and-only globetrotting LD guru himself. By some technological fluke, however, and for reasons I'll probably never understand, I'd been receiving messages politely declining a *previous* request to interview Lavoie, which I'd made... four years earlier!

For some reason, this old email had chosen to appear in my Blackberry as if a daily reminder that I should contact the guy again. I don't know how it started, didn't know how to stop it. But I found it both rather funny and disturbing that a four-year-old rejection email should reappear on the very day we'd agreed to meet.

Lavoie himself found the whole thing rather amusing and had no explanation for this "disquiet ghost in the machine" behaviour either. But I do recall a lot of laughter about it during our interview.

That was just one car in a train of memories that floated through my mind while compiling the essays that form this book. Another was the joy of being able to shake hands with Henry Winkler--"The Fonz" to a generation of TV watchers, "Barry Zuckerkorn" to another. His family playfully referred to him as "the dumb dog" while he was growing up. The 'dumb dog' went on to obtain a Master's degree, create a character that's emerged as a cultural touchstone, and write 19 books.

Much more quietly, perhaps, but no less inspiring is Ron Davis, creator of the Davis Dyslexia Method that's helped thousands of kids globally to shape the management of their dyslexia with a controversial system that's become formally integrated into Iceland's school curriculum. Not bad for someone whose brain was once considered slightly better than a chimpanzee's.

One of the common threads linking most of the inspiring people in this volume is that they are people either living or working with invisible disabilities--in many cases, both. But they're also so much more--they're innovative writers, inspirational teachers, and proud catalysts. They are beautiful human beings who motivate, inspire and sometimes simply rock your world with their stories, theories, dreams, convictions and belief systems.

When people living without a brain-based disability first see the wheelchair, the white cane, the hearing aid, their *first* thought may be what that person *can't* do. With conditions like learning disabilities, ADHD, Asperger's and others, a whole new series of challenges emerge..."Funny.You don't look disabled" is one of the common refrains. And with that a host of criticisms, observations or remarks suddenly rise to the forefront: "He never remembers anything!" "She's always interrupting me!" "If he only applied himself, he'd make magic."

Certainly these were some of the comments I'd heard myself throughout childhood. As an adult, things shifted somewhat in context, but perceptions remained. Without a doubt, one of my all-time favourite performance reviews goes something like this:

"Carter does 80 per cent of an excellent job. The remaining 20 per cent is a trail of destruction the rest of us have to clean up behind him."

A somewhat more tactful, but no less revealing later performance review states that "Carter benefits from verbal reminders."

When I was finally diagnosed with ADHD at the age of 46, there were no surprises but at least I had a context I could frame my behaviours around. "*Oops! Sorry!* Whaddya mean? Most people aren't consistently late for dinner dates?"

"*Oops, sorry!* Seriously, how can your head *not* feel like exploding at this party with like, all these people, loud music and stuff? What? Could you repeat that?"

"*Oops! Sorry!* Whaddya mean you told me you were coming over for coffee last week? Why didn't you remind me?"

"Yes, I know I keep saying 'oops, sorry' a lot... I just can't remember what for!"

It also might help explain how--at the age of 22, after waiting six weeks for the results of a career assessment battery that I'd hung all future hopes on--crushed I felt after being told I'd never be more than a janitor, a coat check attendant--or my personal favourite--a chick sexer, which is decidedly less glamorous than it sounds. (Seriously, look that one up!)

I'll never forget hearing myself say, "This can't be right."

The counsellor leaned forward in her chair. She was one of those people whose glasses threatened to fall off the edge of her nose, so that was what I focused on when she confidently said, "Now you listen to me: I have a master's degree and I *know* what I'm talking about!"

A week later I enrolled in journalism school. A few decades after that I wrote the book you now hold in your hands.

As far as I'm concerned and despite many, many hiccups in life and career, I emerged relatively unscathed.

But this doesn't apply to the estimated 50 percent of female undiagnosed high school dropouts with learning disabilities who wind up pregnant. This doesn't apply to the estimated 50 per cent of incarcerated young men with undiagnosed ADHD. This doesn't apply to the undiagnosed folks who wander hopelessly from job-to-job, spending most of their lives alone in the company of their own fog. This doesn't apply to the unacknowledged souls living disquiet lives who have no emotional vocabulary to describe or any way to manage their condition. This doesn't apply to the ones who can't possibly silence the ceaseless roar of disquiet that only they can hear.

Some will medicate themselves in response. Some will turn to other unhealthy behaviours. Some will drift through life never finding their proper context. Some will be trapped in cultures that perceive their conditions as simply a "white" or "urban" affliction. Study these responses long enough and unhealthy patterns of call-and-response start to emerge. Look deeper still, and you begin to recognize patterns of social consequence that cut deep and distinct.

The gallery of voices assembled in this volume "get it." Their "disquiet" has been channelled into creative works of literature, theatre and visual art. Their disquiet can be reflected in the causes they lend their voices to, whether it's the darkened rooms of sexual abuse, the cultural restrictions of a subject undiscussed or inverting old ways of thinking about language.

This book, then, is a celebration of possibility--of making the invisible, visible. It's a way of honouring the voices heard and the magic that "disquiet" can bring to the unbridled joy of tapping into one's potential and finally discovering the capacity of a path that suddenly materializes before you.

I hope your own path, discovered late and lovely, finally leads you "home."

-Toronto, June 2015

Book of Disquiet

100th Monkey Effect:
The Davis Dyslexia Method

It was only two scant years ago when Tori Jackson found herself, arms
folded, sitting in a chair listening to her mother speaking to yet another
specialist about a curious, too-good-to-be-true-sounding concept to correct
her dyslexia. Jackson, then 11, thought she'd been through it all. Phonics,
tutoring and a host of other interventions had all been tried with only
limited degrees of success. "To say I was skeptical is putting it mildly," the
Grade 9 Halton Region student says. "At first, I thought it was one of my
Mom's crazy new therapy things."

The technique was called Davis Dyslexia Correction and included such
techniques as visualization, playing with clay, and throwing Koosh balls
around. Even Mom thought it sounded rather odd, but after the facilitator
offered a money-back guarantee both mother and daughter decided to take
the proverbial plunge.

"Tori was frustrated," says her mother Karen. "By the time Davis came along, she was feeling like a guinea pig. By the second day, she was making progress. By the end of the week, she was picking up grade-level passages and reading smoothly. When she walked into Grade 8 class, she was reading at a Grade 5 level."

Apparently, "mom's crazy new therapy thing" worked.

Controversial, and certainly unconventional as far as Learning Disability (LD) interventions go, The Davis Dyslexia Correction method first emerged in the early 1980s when its founder, Ron Davis, hit upon a technique of adjusting his own dyslexic perceptions after locking himself in a hotel room for three days, determined to find solutions to problems that had plagued him for years.

Despite wealth, a flourishing artistic career and a successful third marriage, dyslexia had left a crippling life-long imprint on his self-esteem. Unable to speak fully until the age of 17, Davis had endured a childhood populated by schoolyard bullies, "experts" who wanted him institutionalized, physical abuse, rejection from school, the army, his peers. Because of the "dyslexia label", he always felt "less than human", he recalls.

But at the age of 38 -- then a sculptor, the latest in a series of many career jumps – Davis realized that when he was at his artistic best, he was also at his dyslexic worst. On the third day, isolated in his hotel room, he was shocked to realize the letters on the room guest card were actually legible.

"The spaces between the words were there," he says, "And the letters were all the same size. I walked into a library and read *Treasure Island* cover-to-cover. It was exciting, like watching a movie in my head. I got good pictures, which is one of the characteristics of our program. When I saw the story was coming to an end, I noticed a wet spot on the page, another on the end of my nose. I realized I was crying."

The man who had once been labelled as "un-educatable" realized he'd discovered not only a method of reading, but also a way of changing a negative perception of his own life. He shared the method with a dyslexic friend, and before long plunged into the meticulous research that would eventually become a global success story.

"Global" is a good adjective to describe the Davis method. Davis himself claims that many with dyslexia tend to be global observers who think in pictures rather than words, or through self-talk.

Picture thinking is faster than word formulation, and Davis contends that dyslexics have strong imaginations, excel at hands-on activities and creative problem solving. However, they tend to falter with sentence-based, sequential thinking. As problem- solvers, they tend to see issues through three-dimensional multiple viewpoints, turning objects around in their heads. "They are intuitive," he says. "They know the answer without knowing how they got there."

As such, nouns and verbs like "dog", "run" or "mailbox" are easily pictured in the mind's eye, but prepositions, articles, adverbs and conjunctions – words difficult to associate with pictures – tend to lead to what Davis terms "disorientation," a process that can result in classic dyslexia behaviours, including substitutions, omissions, reversals in reading or writing. Davis claims that this phenomenon can also affect auditory processing and motor coordination.

"Old Solutions"

Repeating these errors over and over again not only results in significant loss of self-esteem, but can also lead to a wide range of compulsive behaviours and coping mechanisms to alleviate some of these problems. Thus, rote memorization, illegible handwriting, or avoiding anything relating to reading and writing become "old solutions", as Davis calls them. They begin in childhood and result in a vast arsenal of negative behaviours by the time adulthood is reached. When the disorientation's "trigger" is turned off, reading and spelling problems start improving.

Resolving disorientation caused by auditory symbols – words lacking mental pictures – is the cornerstone of Davis' theory says psychologist

Cathy Dodge Smith, a Davis facilitator for almost a decade and president of the Davis Dyslexia Facilitators' Association of Canada. Smith first stumbled upon the method while speaking to someone who casually asked if she'd read Davis' book, *The Gift of Dyslexia*. Intrigued, Smith obtained a copy and read it. "My jaw dropped. I thought it can't be this simple!" she recalls. Later on, she developed a study at Ryerson University to validate the Davis method. "It was instantly, obviously powerful."

Deciding to take things a step further, Smith enrolled in the Davis training in 1998, quickly moving away from a career as a psychoeducational consultant to becoming a full-time Davis facilitator.

After an initial assessment with a client, facilitators attempt to identify the root of the disorientation, then teach learners how to "turn it off" through relaxation and visualization exercises. "These allow hyperactivity to be brought down to a manageable level and hypoactivity to be brought up to manageable levels," says Smith. "It also allows them to control both their experience and their environment."

Once this is mastered, learners are ready to explore the major blockages: letters of the alphabet, punctuation, and abstract words for which learners have no pictures. Clay becomes a major tool during this process with learners creating two alphabets in both upper-and- lower case.

Learning becomes three-dimensional during this phase with students literally shaping something that's part of them. During this process, facilitators can find letters that trigger disorientation and help the student overcome confusion caused by the letters. Punctuation, the dictionary, reading speed and comprehension are explored using multi-sensory approaches. By engaging the creative process, lasting imagery is embedded in the learner's mind for specific words and letter sequences. Davis facilitators claim the method increases long-term retention without phonetic decoding or memorization. "We work a lot on trigger words," Smith says. "By creating three-dimensional models, using the dictionary and discussing it, we master the meaning of the word. The Davis method identifies over 200 'trigger words' that cause disorientation, including adjectives and prepositions.

"For example, we ask them, 'what does 'of' look like?' Then we might show them a bag of chips and have them make a model to indicate that 'of' means 'containing.' Then we have them look at the word and say, 'this means 'of','" says Smith.

"That's why this program works," Smith enthuses. "We're opening brain pathways to work in harmony."

Perhaps the earliest known reference to any form of "dyslexia" occurs during the 1860s when the German physician, Kussmal, identified that "word blindness" might occur after an insult to the brain, resulting in injuries that affected a person's ability to read, but not to speak or see. Thirty years later another physician, Hinshelwood, after producing several case studies on word blindness, argued that conventional teaching methods were inappropriate for these individuals and endorsed a system relying on a phonetic approach using auditory memory to create words.

Phonics literally made Ron Davis sick. He recalls the upset stomach and migraines that plagued him every time he was subjected to the method during his childhood. This is the man who, at age 12, had his intelligence compared to a chimpanzee's.

"But my mother was an angel," he recalls. She was told I was "uneducateable," but she refused to put me in an institution, although she had no real expectations of me," he says.

His mother did insist he attend regular public schools, which made the young Davis a frequent target of schoolyard bullies, who battled with his older brother who leapt to Ron's defence. Davis' first full sentences were not spoken until he was 17, and with the development of that skill, he learned to cloister his disability by observing others' behaviour. That was also the same year that his IQ tested out at 137.

He did manage to make it into university where he studied architecture. "My reason for going to school was that I wanted to play football," he remembers. "I knew football players went to university, so I thought I'd go too." But his English courses proved too taxing and that, combined with illness, forced him to drop out after two years. He later attempted to enroll in the military and go to Vietnam, but was rejected because of his disability. A girlfriend managed to convince a despondent Davis to apply for a technician's job at the Hercules Powder Company, which produced motors for missiles. "In the 1960s we were in a race with Russia to get to space and you didn't need a degree," says Davis. A series of training courses led to certification as a mechanical engineer. "It's in my blood. I've loved math all my life and being a good engineer has little to do with reading and writing," he proclaims.

A series of technical positions eventually gave way to Davis founding a metal brokerage, which in turn led to a successful real estate career, where he realized enough financial success to retire in his late 30s and then led to his reinvention as a successful artist.

But for all his success, the shadow of his disability chased his footsteps, always making Ron Davis feel "slightly less than human." A year after his breakthrough, Davis co-founded the Reading Research Council, and between 1981 and 1995 approximately 1500 learners, most of them in his native California, received five-day treatment programs. In 1995, the same year as his book, *The Gift of Dyslexia* was published, training became standardized and the Davis Dyslexia Association International was established.

Today, over 450 individuals in 39 countries have become licensed facilitators. Davis methods are used throughout the United States, Germany, The Netherlands and Great Britain. Iceland is moving in the direction of becoming the first country to fully integrate Davis methods into its school system and, in Switzerland some of the treatment program cost is covered under insurance programs.

The program, of course, does have its detractors. Bloggers have claimed his methods are unproven and not scientifically validated, but Davis dismisses this as territorialism. "There's nothing being applied in any LD studies that has true scientific data," he says. "Albert Einstein said that it is the job of science to say 'yes' or 'no'. When you add the human element, all that goes out the window." Cathy Dodge Smith, too, admits that certain pockets in the professional community were resistant to the Davis approach.

"The program's not standard," says Smith. "It requires such a paradigm shift from being a neurological disability, and different thinking from professionals. The method came from one person who was an engineer and has taken a long, long time to reach the mainstream."

"It's just a matter of time before people start catching on," says Davis. "It's that 100th monkey effect, you know, when the 100th monkey gets it, they all do and news travels."

Today, Davis, 65 and proud of his accomplishments, continues to grow his organization. *The Gift of Dyslexia* is now available in 18 languages, and the program has expanded to the point where about 50 percent of all clients have Attention Deficit Hyperactivity Disorder. He continues to be in high demand as an international speaker, and later this year plans to launch a new program aimed at people with autism.

"Right now the biggest problem with the program is who I am," says Davis. "I didn't come from an academic background [that] would have brought credibility. Our greatest credibility exists in the form of satisfied, corrected dyslexics." He is quick to add that, like its founder, his program had its modest beginnings. "It's all right there in the book. I envisioned writing something for parents that a mother of a nine-year-old could teach her child, but it's not closed to anyone."

Perhaps the final verdict rests with young Tori Jackson. "I was amazed. I went through life thinking, 'I'll never be the same as everyone else,' but now I'm not the kid in the corner who has to read with the cassette player anymore."

Tabula Rasa: A Portrait of Dr. Gabor Maté

Whether he's tackling myths surrounding addiction, the intricacies of the mind-body connection or any other controversial topics within his canon, Gabor Maté has been one of my ADHD heroes since publishing his book Scattered Minds *back in 2000. In true ADHD fashion, he's since moved on to a range of literary subjects that have caught his interest and channelled his energies into a series of best-selling books, most recently In the* Realm of Hungry Ghosts: Close Encounters with Addiction, *in which he argues that the origins of addiction reside in early childhood environment. For over a decade he worked in Vancouver's notorious downtown eastside, where the social impact of addiction became a central concern. He has since gone on to co-found* Compassion For Addiction *(www.compassion4addiction.org), a new non-profit aimed treatment and prevention of addiction. He is also an advisor on the fascinating web site http://drugsoverdinner.org/*

He specializes in opening the doors to our own darkened rooms and inviting us in.

In three best-selling books, in columns for *The Globe and Mail* and in his frequent appearances at conferences and workshops across North America, British Columbia-based physician and author Gabor Maté has never shied away from standing in his own truth, even while offering the world his often-controversial views on stress, child rearing, addiction, the mind-body connection or Attention Deficit Hyperactivity Disorder (ADHD).

It is perhaps this last subject for which he is best known. In his first book, *Scattered Minds*, he argues that not enough attention is given to the environmental aspects of ADHD: "I do not see it as a fixed, inherited brain disorder but as a physiological consequence of life in a particular environment, in a particular culture. In many ways one can grow out of it, at any age. The first step is to discard the illness model, along with any notion that medications can offer more than a partial, stopgap response," he wrote.

Response to this, and other assertions, has been greeted with a certain degree of skepticism in some medical circles. But Maté states that the current definition of ADHD given in The American Psychiatric Association's guiding text, *The Diagnostic and Statistical Manual*, "defines ADHD by its external features, not by its emotional meaning in the lives of individual human beings. It commits the faux pas of calling these external observations "symptoms," whereas that word in medical language denotes a patient's own felt experience," he wrote in *Scattered Minds*.

Speaking over the phone from Vancouver, Maté chuckles as he notes the frequency that people misread the title of that book *Scattered Minds*. "A lot of people project into the title and call it 'Shattered Minds'. That's how they read it," he says. "The reality is much more complicated than that. You cannot reduce people to a diagnosis."

Maté writes with a hint of authority on the subject, given that he himself was diagnosed with the condition at age 51.

Furthermore, his three children also live with ADHD. Over the phone, his mercurial mind leaps and bounds from subject to subject. One thought excites another and then it's off to the races on another lively topic. He is passionately lucid when speaking, sometimes abrupt, always engaging.

"I was writing for *The Globe and Mail* when a social worker who had been diagnosed at age 38 contacted me about a possible article on ADHD. Her symptoms described me. "Being diagnosed came as a relief. I saw my own patterns and realized, here's why I couldn't study science earlier; here's why I'm impulsive, disorganized, late. It was a revelation. I had always known something was wrong, but couldn't pinpoint it," he says. "Very little is taught about ADD in medical schools. In retrospect, I missed it in many of my own patients because it wasn't even on my radar.

"Children may have a genetic predisposition to ADHD, but you could argue that ADHD is not genetic. Ninety percent of our brain's circuitry develops in interaction with the environment," he asserts. At birth our head is large and the pelvis is narrow. Horses can walk shortly after birth but we are born immaturely." Other social and environmental factors often play an important role in the mind's healthy development too and the absence of these conditions can have important consequences for healthy brain development. "It's also a problem of society and community and a culture torn asunder by economics," he states. "Look, two parents are often working. Very often the Mom is away, the extended family and community are gone, and children grow up isolated and stressed. Kids don't have optimal brain development under those circumstances."

"Psychiatrists never see normal people!" he exclaims. "They see only people in extreme circumstances. They are not trained in normal human psychological development in medical school. There are no lectures on brain development. The average doctor never hears psychology really; they only study pathology. If a psychiatrist student spends four years in a mental hospital, how are they going to see ADHD as a developmental problem?"

"Social connections lead to neurological connections," is the way psychologist Daniel Seagal once framed it, and this generates a shift to another subject Maté is passionate about and which he feels western medicine largely ignores—the mind-body connection. In *When the Body Says No: Understanding the Stress-Disease Connection*, Maté describes how the hidden stresses resulting from childhood programming and emotional composition can impact on a range of diseases and conditions. He presents evidence that unity exists between the mind and body – including the immune system – and that unhealthy emotional coping patterns learned in early childhood could lead to physical disease.

"The more specialized doctors become, the more they know about a body part or organ and the less they tend to understand the human being in whom that part or organ resides," Maté wrote in *When the Body Says No*, further stating that most of the patients he interviewed for the book revealed that almost none of their doctors had invited them to speak about the subjective and emotional content of their lives. This was further confirmed by dialogues with his medical colleagues who, in the end, knew very little about their patients' lives.

"Socrates stated doctors cannot separate the mind from the body," says Maté, "and our emotions affect the immune system. The heart has a nervous system that has a predictive capacity to it. Our gut has a nervous system which, given its connections with the brain's emotional centres, gives rise to gut feelings of which the conscious mind is inadequately aware. Our conscious mind is only a small part of our 'whole mind' but has little capacity to interpret the world."

He recounts reading a research study about Toronto female breast cancer survivors, who were asked what they thought caused their breast cancer. Many of them identified stress as the trigger. "The women were right: research has a narrow view," he says. "The public is often right. They often know ahead of physicians because they go with their gut rather than box themselves in. Doctors need a different perspective especially when looking at the emotional component of their patients. William Osler is a Canadian doctor still revered today, who was acutely aware of stress-related illness. In the old days we used to have wisdom without science, now we have science without wisdom."

Maté snipes at the western notion of the medical model: "It's about diagnosis and technique. Physicians who intuitively respond to their patients do a whole lot better."

Helping others has always been a key driver in Maté's life. Perhaps part of this motivation to help others stems from the fact he was a child of war. He was born in 1944 in Budapest while under Nazi occupation. His maternal grandparents were killed in Auschwitz when he was five months old. His father was forced into a labour battalion in the service of the German and Hungarian armies. The young Maté was also separated from his mother for a period of time as a way of saving him from death by starvation or disease.

"No great powers of imagination are required to understand that in her state of mind and under the inhuman stresses she was facing daily, my mother was rarely up to the tender smiles and undivided attention a developing infant requires *to imprint a sense of security and unconditional love in his mind," he wrote in When the Body Says No.* "My mother, in fact, told me that on many days her despair was such that only the need to take care of me motivated her to get up from bed. I learned early that I had to work for attention, to burden my mother as little as possible, and that my anxiety and pain were best suppressed."

His own yearnings for a medical career reasserted themselves a few years after he began teaching high school English after graduating with a BA from the University of British Columbia. At 28, he decided to fulfill a lifelong ambition to become a doctor and re-enrolled into University. Upon graduation, he ran a private family practice in East Vancouver for two decades, and was also the Medical Coordinator of the Palliative Care Unit at Vancouver Hospital for seven years. He is currently on staff at the Portland Hotel, a residence for people of Vancouver's eastside where many of his patients live with HIV, mental illness and drug addiction.

At an age when many people have one eye on the horizon of retirement, Maté again reinvented himself, first as a writer for newspapers like *The Globe and Mail* and *Vancouver Sun*, and then as an author. In rapid succession, *Scattered Minds: A New Look at the Origins* and *Healing of Attention Disorder* were published, followed by *When The Body Says No. A* third, *Hold on to Your Kids: Why Parents Need to Matter More Than Peers*, was co-written with psychologist Gordon Neufeld, which dissects parenting from the perspective of attachment theory to illuminate the crucial role parents must play in the upbringing of their children. All three books have been national best-sellers.

Maté currently maintains a rigorous touring schedule to support the demands of those requesting speaking engagements. He continues his role on staff at The Portland Hotel while working on a new book, *Chasing The Dragon: Close Encounters With Addiction.*

Despite this flurry of activity, Maté shows no signs of slowing down, committed in his wisdom and his want to helping others. "I've always wanted to make a contribution," he says. "Much of that is shaped by being a child of genocide. I've learned that people need to be more human and society needs to be humane. Nobody should stay silent."

Best Before Date

As the Washington-based National Association of Social Workers gears up for implementing the latest criteria and codes of everyone's favourite psychiatric reference bible the DSM 5, in October 2015, we have learned that the world didn't implode upon its publication by the American Psychiatric Association in 2013. The latest edition certainly wasn't without its share of controversy: Asperger Syndrome was dropped as a distinct classification; "gender identity disorder" was re-christened "gender dysphoria" and the A2 criterion for post-traumatic stress disorder was also dropped, among other significant revisions. Critics have attacked the latest edition as being poorly written, lacking in empirical support, and perhaps most damningly, filled with conflict-of-interest accusations, since over 69 per cent of the DSM task force reported having ties to the pharmaceutical industry. Criticism of the latest edition finally manifested in the form of a petition with over 13,000 signatories that called for a rigorous outside review of the book. This article written during the mounting anxiety expressed by service providers in anticipation of the DSM 5, attempted to dissect the risks and benefits of actually applying labels on people with disabilities and what the meaning of those labels actually implied.

E ver since 1840 when the American Census first included a question on idiocy/insanity, mental health professionals have been trying to put a label on things. Matters are about to get a lot worse.

With a scheduled 2013 launch, the fifth edition of that controversial psychiatrist's bible, the makers of *The Diagnostic and Statistical Manual (DSM)* are currently reviewing all kinds of disorders you've never heard of that are vying for inclusion. Conditions such as "Internet Addiction," "Apathy Syndrome" and "Parental Alienation Disorder" are in direct competition with the better-known but not-yet-included "Fetal Alcohol Syndrome" and "Seasonal Affective Disorder."

Published by The American Psychiatric Association, the most recent version of the DSM clocks in at over 900 pages and includes almost 300 disorders, from mild mental retardation—itself a dated term—to depression, and a personal favourite, "cognitive disorder not otherwise specified."

Small wonder then that the tome has come under fire by critics who argue that some disorders listed are either cultural or imagined in nature. Homosexuality, once listed as a mental health disorder itself, was finally dropped in 1973. At a briefing in February, some psychiatrists winced at the possible inclusion of labels like, "Psychosis Risk Disorder," arguing that everyone was at risk of being labelled with something.

Others charge that the DSM is too heavily influenced by avaricious pharmaceutical companies looking to make a profit from the latest diagnostic craze. Indeed, medication sales for drugs treating ADHD, autism and childhood bipolar disorder exploded after the definitions were expanded in the most recent DSM that was published in 1994. In the United States alone, sales for ADHD medications topped $4.8 billion in 2008.

There have always been arguments against labelling children. "Labels are for jelly jars" chimes psychologist and writer Lynne Namka who once wrote: "Labelling is definitive; once we say it, then it holds meaning. The danger of labels is that children tend to believe what is said about them and live up to that negative expectation. Negative labels keep children caught in negative behaviour. Labelling what we do not know how to deal with is victimization."

Some, like psychologist Carol Dweck, have conducted studies on gifted students and found that their motivation to take on challenging assignments actually decreases when praised for their intelligence, thus pleading a case that labelling can also affect academic motivation.

And while it is probably true that yesterday's "quirky" child is today's pathologized child, labels, especially those used constructively, can provide a useful framework for treating legitimate disorders. Furthermore, the appropriate label is necessary to obtain insurance and funding for treatment, and often, access to service providers.

"Bureaucracy requires the label in order to fund services," says Toronto psychologist and artist Michael Irving, who designed the well-received Child Abuse Monument. "Labels can help us understand what is going on as service providers, and can help the child understand themselves and get more positive. Labelling needs to be helpful to the child and we need to see the positive and communicate it."

Ottawa psychologist, Judy Goldstein, concurs. "The label helps us (service providers) take the right direction and identify the proper intervention that will help. Everyone is an individual and not everyone needs the same intervention. It helps us look at the whole person and use the diagnosis as part of the puzzle to understand the person," she says.

But a diagnosis can be difficult to understand, especially if criteria differentiates from source-to-source, as sometimes happens with learning disabilities (LD), for example.

"I prefer the terms 'learning differences' or 'learning styles' suggests another Ottawa psychologist, Brian MacDonald, co-founder of www.familyanatomy.com. "'Learning disabilities' is the term recognized by schools and physicians, but I'm careful to define it for parents and kids because I think it's a misleading term."

It helps when definitions complement each other. For example, The Learning Disabilities Association of Ontario's definition of LD is frequently cited throughout Canada. In part it states that LDs are "a variety of disorders that affect the acquisition, retention, understanding, organization or use of verbal and/or non-verbal information. These disorders result from impairments in one or more psychological processes related to learning (a), in combination with otherwise average abilities essential for thinking and reasoning."

MacDonald is quick to point out that this is different from the DSM's definition, which identifies problems with reading, math and written expression, "but the DSM looks at achievement vs. intelligence. "If you look at a child who spends three hours a night doing homework, but his peers are taking only one hour to do the same volume of work and achieving at the same level, those kids wouldn't meet the criteria to qualify for a label of learning disability," he says.

Sometimes labels are vague enough to fall into a completely different category of disability. For example, anxiety frequently mimics symptoms such as the restlessness, impulsiveness and inattentiveness often associated with Attention Deficit Hyperactivity Disorder. Two diagnoses that frequently and erroneously cross back and forth are those for non-verbal learning disabilities and Asperger's Syndrome, a "higher-functioning" form of autism. These disabilities often involve excellent verbal skills, but may also include problems with mathematics, visual spatial processing and social perception.

"Both of these disabilities have social problems for very different reasons," says Judy Goldstein. "There is some overlap, but kids with Asperger's may get caught in something and repeat it over and over, but a non-verbal wouldn't do that. A student with non-verbal learning disabilities might have problems in school with spatial perception, but no such problems with Asperger's. You have to look at strengths, weaknesses and symptoms," she says.

There are some who argue that both disabilities are one and the same, but there is no conclusive proof of this--another situation where labels given responsibly by a qualified psychologist can clearly help. All the psychologists interviewed also agreed that a psychodiagnostic assessment, while helpful, isn't nearly enough. There have to be solutions and recommendations for accommodations, so strategies can be implemented to suitably monitor and manage the disability accordingly.

"It's important that parents and students have an awareness of the specific nature of the problem, not just some overall view of the problem, like, say 'anxiety'." says MacDonald. "But what does it mean specifically for that person? That gives a starting point to find strategies that will be helpful." He cites an example of an Ottawa teacher who noticed several students were having problems remembering concepts on a particular subject.

"The teacher worked with the class to brainstorm the areas they were having difficulty in remembering and then had them write each item down on 4X6 index cards. These were put into a portable format and personalized so the students could use the information on a day-to-day basis and for tests, which is much more like the real world."

The teacher took an identified—or labelled—problem, in this case, memory, and found positive results when the class collectively took ownership of their situation and wound up with a positive outcome. And it's the positivity that's critical for finding a successful solution when dealing with negative behaviours, says Michael Irving. "If a child is bull-headed, you might want to say he has tenacity," he says. "In using a label, realize that-protection. You have to ask, what is the intent behind the behaviour?"

"Realize that there's an external response in a problem behaviour and there's likely a positive root as some form of self-protection. So, we have to say, "it's really great that you're trying to protect yourself, but now we have to ask, what is a more successful way of taking care of yourself? What's going on inside so you don't have to arrive at the place where bad stuff is going on?"

When placed in a positive context, a label, in fact, can be tremendously empowering for people. It can provide a kind of blue print for treatment, offer an understanding and ownership of a particular challenge. Likewise, it can form the basis for a "healing partnership" between client and support team as the labelled person can formulate strategies for later success. "We have to switch to labels that help understand the positive forces behind problematic behaviours," says Irving. "At that point we have to shift the label to the positive to serve the child, and not the teacher or the system."

Batteries Not Included:
Getting Motivated with Rick Lavoie

One of my LD heroes, writer Rick Lavoie, has never shied away from rattling people's perceptions of learning disabilities during an illustrious four decade career. Indeed, the former residential programs administrator for children with special needs has successfully carved out a new career for himself as author and speaker. Best known for the in-your-face F.A.T. City workshops, he continues to travel the globe challenging and inspiring. This story was written following a memorable dinner that wouldn't have happened if Lavoie's email had anything to say about it!

F or over three decades Rick Lavoie has been raising eyebrows – and sometimes dropping jaws – with his tactics for increasing awareness of learning disabilities, especially in children. Perhaps best known for his F.A.T. City workshop videos, the in-your-face workshops that shocked people into recognizing learning disabilities, and recent books, including *It's So Much Work to Be Your Friend*, he has addressed over half a million people through his fast-paced interactive lectures throughout North America, Australia and Hong Kong.

Lavoie's career has recently taken a different turn with the publication of his latest tome, *The Motivation Breakthrough: 6 Secrets for Turning On the Tuned Out Child*. He's quick to point out, in his inimitable style, that he dislikes the book's title, noting that the publisher insisted on it.

But how many times have you heard refrains like, "He's so bright...if he only learned to apply himself." "She just doesn't seem to care." "He can do it if he just puts his mind to it." Lavoie says that traditionally, kids have been motivated two ways: either through reward or punishment. Neither way is particularly good.

Typically kids are assigned all the responsibility for learning, and the teacher is assigned none. "It's like the used car salesman who says there are no motivated buyers...well, that's his job," Lavoie cracks. "Sometimes professionals are obstacles on the journey," he adds.

Amassing stacks of research in search of new motivational models when he sat down to write the book, Lavoie was surprised to discover that some of the best and most successful models came out of the business world. "Some of it is impeccably done," he says. "So we reviewed what Madison Ave. had done, and put together and adapted some strategies for parents and teachers."

One of the key messages to emerge from that research was that "success works" he says. "Educators don't get that, but business has long gotten it. Employers are constantly motivating employees with even simple ideas like 'Employee of the Month'. They understand that success builds on success."

Lavoie argues that a key motivating factor for kids means that an update in teaching style for most educators is required. He points out that out of 17,500 entries in the *World Book Encyclopaedia*, 17,400 entries needed updating, emphasizing that the world is constantly changing.

"It's no longer appropriate to teach the kid stuff," he says. "Teach them how to learn stuff." The book examines and counters several myths on motivation, including the old stand-by, "He's so lazy, he won't even try." Lavoie points out that the laziness is actually learned helplessness, emphasizing that the two look exactly the same.

Another myth is the concept of competition with peers. This reflects deficits in the motivation theory as well because the only child who will be motivated by competition is the child who feels he has a chance at winning.

For kids with learning disabilities and ADHD, Lavoie points out that making successes measurable is a huge factor in successful motivation. "Our kids don't get implied messages, they need to hear, 'I love you,' " he says. Furthermore, it's necessary to make success visible, whether it's through a chart on the fridge or something else that's tangible.

What's more, he states that kids with LD/ADHD frequently have issues with executive functions.

"They can't prioritize, which is huge in motivation and a key factor in many success stories," he points out. "So sometimes we have to teach the child what motivates them. This is also the root of good self-advocacy.

"People tend to view executive problems as a symptom when in fact it's a cause. If we can teach the child better executive strategies, he'd be more motivated."

Lavoie is quick to point out that whether living with learning disabilities or not, people will be motivated if their needs are met. And, like Maslow's famous Hierarchy of Needs theory, people are motivated to succeed by certain needs, including:

• Status (the need to feel important)
• Inquisitiveness (the need to know and learn)
• Application (the need to be associated with something larger than yourself)
• Power (the need for control and authority)
• Aggression (the need to be assertive)
• Autonomy (the need to be independent)
• Achievement (the need for recognition) and
• Gregariousness (the need to belong)

The book offers several strategies to meet these needs, organized into The Six P's: People, Prestige, Prizes, Projects, Praise and Power.

Many strategies, like "The Minor Choice Technique" are relatively easy to employ. "You're asking the child to write a 200-word essay about a dog and he's argumentative, so you offer him a choice between writing the essay on white or yellow paper. By giving them a choice, you are giving them a sense of power," he says, and making them a participant in the decision-making process. This is important when, as colleague Mel Levine established, adolescence is a "24-hour, 365-day battle not to be embarrassed."

That's just another anecdote that comes flying out of Lavoie's mouth--one of thousands-- that have been accumulated over a 30-year career that included various administrator and management roles in residential programs for children. In an illustrious career, he's amassed three degrees in Special Education, been awarded two Honorary Doctorates in Education, served as a lecturer at numerous universities, including Harvard and The University of Alabama. The books, workshops and videos that he has accumulated are a testament to his popularity as an in-demand speaker.

While the new book has been generally well-received, it's been attacked by teachers in some quarters who scoff that Lavoie's techniques won't work in overstuffed classrooms. Lavoie, however, argues that teaching in a closed book format won't prepare kids for an open book world, and teachers have to accept more responsibility for the diversity of learning styles in front of them.

"We're in a different time, educating for a different time," he says flatly. "The world has never been more different than when we were educated."

Dispatches From The Short Bus:
A Talk with Jonathan Mooney

Once told he would never be anything more than a dishwasher, author Jonathan Mooney has not only come to terms with his cognitive differences, but he also graduated from an Ivy League university and now aims for nothing less than a learning revolution.

I t's an election year in the United States, and Jonathan Mooney wants you to start rethinking education. He wants to replace the "chalk-and-talk" days of yesteryear with more individualized narrowcast learning, where the "sage on the stage" is a facilitator and learning is largely inquiry-based.

High goals indeed for the highly-regarded author of the acclaimed book, *The Short Bus*. "Schools prepare generalists for a world of specialists," he says. "About 85 per cent of all jobs use only Grade 8 math, but require degrees." Mooney states the time is right to re-imagine the future of education in which he sees Attention Deficit Disorder (ADD) as strength-based and student-centred.

The premise is that America has been having the educational reform conversation, which is about performance and teacher evaluations and so on, but it's not about the most important thing: learning reform." He sees the current state of education as a 19th century approach in a 21st century world.

"Folks learn when education is relevant to their lives and when they have chosen their own educational path," he emphasizes. Much of this is the thrust of a new book—his third--*Redrawing the Lines: Dispatches From the Front Line of the Learning Revolution*, which re-imagines where education can go, and the changes it must make if it is to remain relevant and impactful.

The book may have its roots in the missing pieces of his own childhood education. Diagnosed with dyslexia and ADHD at age eight, he started making inroads towards reading by age 12. "I was pretty much a text book case when it came to dyslexia," he says. "I don't really read well and in the traditional grammatical sense, I'm not that good at writing either."

He recalls with a touch of sadness in his voice how, as a child, the expectation was for him to sit still in class. Unfortunately, it wasn't long before his ADHD dropped in to say hello for the day. "Pretty soon both feet would be bouncing, and after about 30 minutes, I'd bust out the drums. About a minute later, I'd be trying to wrap my leg behind my neck. Pretty shortly after I'd be sent down to the principal's office." He spent so much time sitting outside of the principal's office that he became good buddies with the school janitor. But the messaging received from the experience was a little more dire.

"If you don't sit still, you're a bad kid. The cultural norms were, if you didn't read, you were considered a dumb kid. I was in the slow reading group--*See Spot Run* and all that. Half the time I'd be making fun of my situation; the other half of the time I'd be hiding in the bathroom to avoid reading out loud." It's a fascinating paradox then, that the kid who didn't want to read *See Spot Run*, was not only accepted into an ivy league school, but also went on to major in English Literature. He accounts for the irony in two ways.

"One is kind of pragmatic," he says. "I was gonna prove people wrong and show that I could work at the highest level and graduate with a 4.0. The other more important reason is that my strengths were storytelling, ideas. I was supported by a range of teachers from Grade 3 all the way into college and encouraged to engage in the logistics of literature. I had teachers who said I could engage in the highest levels of literature even if I didn't read. They handed me books on tape and said, go learn it.

Even though my reading and writing weren't great, I had other strengths—thinking and understanding—that I could do well." He has stated that he believes his kind of challenges are largely context-driven. "The same trail that gets you into trouble in school is the same stuff that helps you succeed in the corporate context."

And succeed, he has. As a consultant, he's worked with Exxon and The United Way and helped them to realize the benefits of neurodiversity in the workplace by facilitating groups and nurturing youth development. He's also the co-founder with Bill Flink, of a national, non-profit mentoring program, Project Eye-to-Eye, which has paired thousands of high school kids with Learning Disabilities (LDs) and ADHD with college students who act as role models, mentors and guides. The wildly successful program has been steadily growing over the years with chapters in well over a dozen states.

"The holy grail of this work is positive self-concept," he says. "A parent can tell their kid is smart, but they're the wrong messenger. The program's vision is pretty simple," he continues. "The idea is that young people who are going through a hard school experience need a positive vision of the future. The natural way to do that seemed to bring living, breathing role models together with younger people. The program strives to give hope through mentoring."

But mentoring is just one component in a future ripe with educational possibilities. Mooney points to charter schools as one potential model. We chat about individualized and applied degrees before the conversation turns to technology's role in educating kids with LDs.

"Technology allows a classroom to be flipped. The traditional model emphasized time broadcasting information with a minimal amount of time applying that. It allows the "... the holy grail of this work is positive self-concept ..." "... the time is right to re-imagine the future of education ..." student to work according to their learning style and at their own pace. It also frees the teacher up to connect with students and frees them to facilitate an inquiry-based learning experience where real learning happens."

And that's perhaps Mooney's greatest focus right now: nothing less than a complete learning revolution that's student-focused, inquiry-based and future-viewing. "The emphasis has always been on "fix the kid, not the environment," says Mooney. "Our big challenge is to change the dominant way we educate young people. We need a learning revolution."

Disguised, Denied, Dismissed or Diminished:
Cross-Cultural Experiences of LD

This one was written while sick and feeling sorry for myself following surgery. Can't help but wonder if some of that crept into the piece here-and-there. Nonetheless, it's a topic I'd been wanting to explore again ever since publishing a book, Benchmarking, *back in 2005. We'd included a chapter on this topic back then, but I never felt it was explored properly. One of the nice aspects of living in a city like Toronto—a place I never get tired of complaining about—is its diversity. That includes the various sub-cultures of people living with invisible disabilities I've met along the way. I'm especially grateful to my friend Darrel Kane Gladue for introducing me to his warrior-mama Mabel, herself a pioneering social worker who offered to share her story for this essay.*

Every day Mabel Nipshank wakes up with gratitude. Every day Mabel Nipshank thanks her creator for blessing her with gifts. It's quite a change from the feelings she had as a child growing up. The 64-year-old, Vancouver-based, shelter support worker had always thought she was stupid.

"I grew up in a Métis village of about 300 people in northern Alberta. I struggled and wouldn't apply for jobs that involved thinking," she says. "I thought the only thing I had to offer was my looks.

"I was articulate and grew up speaking Cree. My grandparents would say I was smart and I would pick up things, but in a school setting things were different. All the kids would tease me."

Somehow, she managed to cope and learned to get by with her reading and writing challenges. Then, after returning to school in her 40's, an instructor identified her struggle by name: dyslexia.

"I was never ashamed about not 'getting' something. If she (the instructor) said it out loud, I would get it. She said I was an audio learner.

"I have a hard time reading columns. Tables as well," she says. "I have a hard time reading recipes or anything with a 'tail'. And I'm a horrible, horrible speller! Spell Check is the best thing that ever came out for me. At work, when documenting activity for the day, she "double-and-triple checks everything."

Proud of her culture, Nipshank points to the rich oral traditions that formed such a deep part of her Cree heritage.

"It really shaped me," she says. "Elders teach you in a way you have to figure out yourself, by storytelling. If my grandmother caught me doing something wrong, she'd sit me down and tell me a story so I'd figure the problem out."

And storytelling, perhaps, was the bridge between the oral traditions of her culture and auditory processing for Nipshank. Both played to her learning and processing strengths. Indeed, visual processing and spatial relations appeared to be at the root of her learning struggles. In this case, Nipshank believes that her cultural belief systems played an active role in helping her cope.

"My culture has always been accepting of difference," she says. "And as more studies surface regarding disabilities, there's definitely more sensitivity and more of a push towards different methods of teaching."

This is certainly not the case across all cultures. Because of its invisibility, learning disabilities (LDs) and ADHD are often hard to detect. Easily misinterpreted, LDs might be perceived as a mental health condition or laziness or an intellectual disability. Furthermore, they might be seen as a "white" or "urban" condition.

"I have worked with individuals with learning disabilities, and families where one or more members have a learning disability from both collectivist and individualistic cultures. If the individual has been diagnosed with a learning disability, it is typically perceived as an intellectual deficit that acts as an obstacle to learning, school success, and relationships with family and friends along with future success. The learning disability is often seen as "unfair" and unique to the individual/family. For those involved in educational systems unfamiliar with or unprepared for students with learning disabilities, they are often greatly frustrated by the lack of understanding and services available to them," says doctor of education and Ryerson University instructor, Audrey Huberman.

A 1998 study by Selway and Ashman claims that German and Australian communities are most accepting of learning disabilities, followed by English, Italian, Chinese, Greek and Arabic communities. Other stats, however, suggest that "families who see disability as a punishment for past wrongs may be reluctant to seek intervention for loved ones with LD. (Wong, 2005) It's no secret that racist undertones, however subtle, can flow throughout the attitudes of a dominant culture, as well. Visible minorities with disabilities wind up often paying the price in a systemic context.

The National Association for the Education of African American Children with Learning Disabilities (AACLD) references 2008 statistics on its web site and states: "although African Americans represented just 15% of all students, they represented 21% of students in the special education category of specific learning disabilities, 29% in the category of emotional disturbance and 31% in the category of mental retardation." The web site further goes on to say that there is a huge discrepancy in the drop-out rates between minority children with disabilities and white children.

The condition may also be hidden from others in the family, and this can have devastating consequences, says Dr. Huberman. "An individual with a learning disability from a collectivist culture may experience conflict around issues of identity, inclusion, and belonging. Collectivist cultures differ from individualist cultures in their tendency to value and promote the needs of the whole over its parts. Individuals with diverse abilities, needs and behaviours, such as those with learning disabilities can present as obstacles to the collective framework. Therefore individual differences may be disguised, denied, dismissed and diminished. The individual may be left to experience shame, marginalization, exclusion, and an incomplete sense of belonging and cultural identity. S/he is denied the interventions and accommodations that lead to individual and collective success."

****

One day Cindy Wang, a Chinese social worker, now 37, asked her mother how she had explained her daughter's non-verbal learning disability and ADHD to the rest of the family.

"She said there is no language for it and that is very telling in a cultural context," says Wang.

"The closest thing is to describe someone as 'slow' or with a genetic deficiency or incapable of learning. There is no distinction made between Down syndrome and central auditory processing disorder--not even acknowledging that there is such a thing!

"My uncle, who is in his 70s, once said to my mother, 'well this obviously comes from your side of the family.' Since then, there have been some signs of similar conditions within younger members of the family, so my uncle keeps quiet. He does try his best and tries to be more sensitive now. Whenever he sees me, he refers to it as 'your condition' but still can't name what I have."

"Unfortunately, individualist cultures, while comfortable with individual differences, are often equally uncomfortable with "disability" as are collective cultures. However [it's] due to reasons of personal discomfort rather than concerns around the collective good. Resolving the problems that arise from a culture's discomfort with "difference" regardless of the reason -- personal or collective -- rests in the cause of the problem. Therefore, cultural frameworks require re-adjustment. When collectivist cultures reframe individual differences to opportunities for novel perspectives, those with learning disabilities can receive the support they need and contribute to the collective. When individualistic cultures reframe disability to "different ability", barriers can diminish and new opportunities, lifestyles and economies can develop. This reframing is essential. Denial, disguising, dismissing and diminishing rarely work for long as learning disabilities do not hide themselves or go away with time. However, with proper support they certainly can be compensated and accommodated" says Huberman.

Accessing support is definitely one step towards resolving the situation. But some cultures engage in behaviours perceived as "normal," which may in fact be seen as inappropriate or even pathological through other eyes. Other complications can include elements such as differing diagnostic criteria and rating systems. The standard reference in North America, for example, is of course, the *Diagnostic Statistical Manual*, an update of which is due for publication later this year. In the United Kingdom, however, the International Classification of Diseases (ICD-10) criteria is more restrictive. It may also explain lower rates of ADHD (for example) in the UK than in the States.

Of further interest is a 2008 study where Lebanese teachers and parents were presented with vignettes of kids with different ADHD subtypes and asked to describe the behaviours they observed. The teachers did not observe any medical conditions and many of the parents identified the behaviours as being positive when the child was a boy. Therefore, "the recognition of ADHD symptoms and the labelling of distress as being deviant or pathological depend on the norms behaviour accepted in a particular culture," noted Rousseau et al (2008).

So, it seems reasonable to suggest that LDs and ADHD (and possibly other invisible disabilities) are contextual, and depends on a variety of sociocultural variables and the individual's relationship with them. Nonetheless, the individual must learn appropriate coping and supportive strategies, and accommodations must take the environment into account when treatment is offered or available.

The sociocultural perspective is rather new, but it does open up new avenues for analysis and insights into attitudes of some cultural groups regarding LDs and ADHD. It also broadens the biological and medical perspectives that have, until now, been the primary methods used for research in this area. And even that has been rather scant.

****

A 2008 story published online in *Proceedings of the National Academy of Sciences,* suggested neurological differences in the way Chinese and English speakers processed information. The study found that English speakers tended to have "functional abnormalities" in the back parts of the brain associated with reading.

On the other hand, Chinese speakers with dyslexia tended to have brain abnormalities in both function and structure related to reading in the left-middle-frontal region of the brain.

The research is based on brain scans performed on 16 Chinese speakers with dyslexia and 16 of their peers with normal reading ability during the course of a couple of tests. The researchers explained that the Chinese language uses characters while English uses a letter alphabet. "At the functional level, it's easy to understand why Chinese and English speakers use different parts of the brain to read language," says Li-Hai Tan, a professor of linguistics and neuroscience at the University of Hong Kong and author of the paper.

"The different brain networks accommodate the different features of English and Chinese. The two systems are dramatically different. Chinese is pictographic and English is more phonological, or sound-based." But he says that it is striking that the Chinese children with dyslexia had less grey matter in the middle-frontal gyrus, and that was probably a function of genetics, since this phenomenon is thought to be largely genetic. This would suggest that the genetic makeup of Chinese speaking children with dyslexia is different from that of English speakers with the same disorder since they have reductions of grey matter in different sites of the brain

A 2004 study published in *Nature* magazine suggested that learning Chinese creates specific demands on the human brain for remembering visual patterns. English readers tend to utilize areas for phoneme processing. The ability to (analyze) process syllables into phonemes—the smallest unit of linguistic measurement to convey meaning or distinction of a word in any given language--is a key issue in dyslexia, suggest researchers Joey Tang and Brian Butterworth.

They contend that reported dyslexia rates are higher in English (approximately five per cent) than in Chinese. Returns on a Beijing survey of 8000 school children indicated that 1.5% were dyslexic. In his study, Butterworth argued for a universal basis in the brain that affects phonemic analysis. Tan, however concluded that "the biological abnormality of impaired reading is dependent on culture."

If anything, the research suggests that there is much more work yet to be done.

Solutions?

"Five-to-seven years ago, the world was a different place," says Rondon Rollocks, a special events project manager living with dyslexia and ADHD. "Dragon and other apps weren't around. It was a completely different world and now my life has opened up."

As an Afro-Canadian growing up in Toronto, Rollocks didn't know he was dyslexic. Simple things seemed impossible.

"I was always labelled as having "potential." None of the testing I ever did identified me as 'dyslexic.'" But, he notes, at 16 or 17, he didn't possess the fundamentals in grammar that would allow him to go further. "In high school, I kept going for extra help but was told I lost the chance to go to university."

His reading is very slow and he says he has to look at the shape of the word to determine what it is. "My brain looks at word shapes instead of processing phonetically."

Despite these challenges, he has done well, establishing himself as a prominent entrepreneur with a host of accommodations and the ability to delegate at least to some people, tasks he finds difficult to perform. He has been successful in part because of a sprawling network and a supportive family.

"I came from an exceptional family that has done well. I don't have an accent and I'm very confident. I don't think my experience is typical because I've always done well. Also, growing up middle class offered access to money and to power."

Which is great if you have acquired knowledge and ownership of your LD. But the denial of LDs and ADHD by some cultures has implications for the Canadian workforce. Current annual immigration levels hover at around 250,000 people. If we're to accept that about 10 per cent of the population has some form of LD, this means that approximately 25,000 people with potential LDs are settling into the country every year.

In her 2002 workshop on *ESL Speakers with LD,* Robin Schwarz identified several reasons why the presence of LD might be misidentified or harder to detect in ESL speakers. Behaviours that may be perceived as normal or possibly even healthy, such as speaking out of turn and rote learning in some cultures may in fact suggest LD in North American culture. Furthermore, phenomena such as culture shock, poor health, gender status and behaviour, poverty, and separation from family can all have an impact on learning.

"Unfortunately, the current point system, suggests that Canada values "able" immigrants over those less able. The "indicators" that an applicant may have a learning disability overlap those of poverty, minority status, lack of education and opportunity. Therefore, to prevent the further mistreatment and disempowerment of those on the margins--women, those with mental illness, the poor and uneducated along with individuals with learning disabilities and/or a physical disability--an immigration system based on a commitment to inclusion rather than "ability" is required," says Audrey Huberman.

Fortunately, a greater sensitivity to the needs of minorities, early intervention and identification strategies, an awareness of differing learning models through universal education and other strategies are slowly emerging—albeit at a glacial pace—to assist people from various cultures.

For Rondon Rollocks, the focus has shifted from "culture" to "communication." People (in organizations like the workplace) just want to get their message across," he says. "We're looking for common ground to get the message out and people just want a clear way to communicate. There are many different reasons why people can't understand. At some point the message has to shift to a place where the meaning becomes more clear, such as walking people through a combination of steps to convey information. It's time consuming, yes, but the alternative is chaos."

Still, others aren't so fortunate and have to sometimes choose between obtaining help or risk being shamed by a culture that doesn't understand or accept invisible disabilities.

Cindy Wang points out that, coming from a collectivist culture, "it takes a person with enormous will power and a strong self-esteem to get support, regardless of community acceptance. You need to find your network, your community and support elsewhere, if you have to," she says, with a slightly exasperated sigh.

And once that support has been accessed, it can be transformative, says Dr. Huberman.

"As a helping professional, I rarely see individuals or families that deny a learning disability or any other issue. While they may call it something else or not know what it is, a problem has been acknowledged--an essential first step in seeking help. In my experience, once the family and/or the individual has come for help, a conversation around explaining and normalizing a learning disability is possible and can lead to the understanding that their learning disability is "manageable" and even the underlying cause of the personal qualities that they are proud of."

Lesley Andrew: Go Big or Go Home

Within the culture of disability, the sub-culture of people labelled gifted LD have always been given short shrift. They're too intelligent to be considered "disabled" yet too disabled to be part of the mainstream. Indeed, it's almost as if it's a disability-within-a disability. Still, singer-actor Lesley Andrew has faced those challenges directly, inverting the term on its head while actually making a living as a Canadian artist. I first heard her inspiring tale at an LDAO fundraising breakfast a few years ago. She continues to teach, perform and inspire.

O ur interview begins with a joke:

Q: *What's the difference between a Canadian musician and a pizza?*

A: *A pizza can feed a family of four.*

This is the humour that's kept singer-actor Lesley Andrew in high demand throughout her career. It's also the type of biting wit that liberally peppers her highly-rated and in-demand motivational speeches. She's had extended runs at Stratford appearing in productions ranging from *The Mikado* and *Twelfth Night* to *Patience*. She's recorded three CDs full of well-received jazz music, answered the calls of people like Jay Leno, Oprah Winfrey, and Donny and Marie. She's wowed 'em during tours of Europe, Canada, the United States and Argentina. She's done all that and continues to perform, teach, adjudicate and direct shows as well. "As an artist it's either feast-or- famine in Canada," she cracks. Normally 'on hiatus' which means 'unemployed.' To survive, you either have to be specific or go the diverse route. I chose to go diverse," she says.

"When I started acting, people were surprised that I also sang. Likewise, they were surprised that I was also an actor. We have a tendency to put people into little boxes, but as long as you have a good story, you're good to go." It wasn't always that easy though. It's an attitude that's been cultivated only after years of practice and training. A rarified creature indeed, Andrew was diagnosed as Gifted LD only while attending high school in Milton ON, an experience she describes as "pretty horrible."

"During public school we had an open pod concept, which means there were no walls." Given that her LDs affect her auditory processing, that must have been difficult to say the least. Andrew also lives with dyslexia, 'and all the other 'ics' as well," she jokes. "I didn't know my times tables and was terrible at math."

Reading music was also difficult for her, although she developed a method for overcoming this too. To this day she struggles with concepts that are unrelated to each other--lists, for example.

The giftedness was in some ways as big a burden. "For a while I could use the giftedness to cover the LD," she says, "but people assume you're faking the LD." Part of compensating for her was learning to exploit her differences.

"As a musician you make your living standing out in a crowd. And hey, I'm 5' 10" with curly red hair. So I capitalized on it. You either go big or go home." Despite her success, in true Canadian style, she still auditions for parts.

"Success for me is never having to audition," she says. "But this is the age of technology and that hinders performers. As an artist you can't rest on your laurels. You have to prove yourself over and over again."

So she moves between opera and operetta, classical and jazz. "I sing whatever pays the mortgage." Some of these stories are shared in her popular "Beating the Odds" workshops, which she frequently gives at conferences and appearances around the province. "I cover things like being responsible for your time, being rewards-driven not consequence-driven and being positive," she says. It's a formula that appears to have worked and carries over into her messages about living well with learning disabilities.

"You've got to hang in there and choose friends who are going to support you, be willing to make decisions and live with the results of that decision. Are you going to grow your nails or bite them? The value is in your difference and that's what makes you beautiful."

For more information, visit Lesley Andrew's website at www.dreaminprogress.com

Rick Green: Dancing With One Leg Shorter

Funny guy Rick Green has emerged as one of my favourite ADHD people in recent years. He's had a stellar career as a comedian, married the lovely and spiritual Ava who serves as administrator, co-creator, muse and protector of his time and talent; managed to carve a solid and vital niche for himself with two insightful and hysterical documentaries that turn the perception of ADHD on its head. It's all done tongue-in-cheek in a way that's both funny and respectful of its subject. That's hard to achieve but he's done it. Currently working on a new documentary about ADHD in the workplace, Green remains an accessible and quintessentially Canadian commentator on all things ADHD. After confirming him to speak at a recent conference we were organizing, he quipped, "I can hardly wait to find out what I'm going to say!" That's both very Rick and very ADHD.

W ikipedia got it all wrong: Rick Green is alive and kicking, and wrapping up a new documentary, thank you very much.

The Canadian actor-writer-director, perhaps best known for his work on the long-running comedy series *The Red Green Show*, got a chuckle months ago when the citizen-owned online encyclopaedia greatly exaggerated rumours of his demise by announcing his premature death.

"Several people were actually rather upset by it," Green chuckles over the phone. "But the mistake's been corrected. So, I'm still alive."

If anything, it's Rick Green's aliveness that makes him such an engaging conversationalist: the passion when he speaks about his ADHD; it's impact on his life as an artist and the child-like joy of discovery, as he describes some of the content of his upcoming documentary *ADD and Loving It?!* airing on Global Television this Fall.

Hosted by Canadian funny guy –and frequent Green collaborator—Patrick McKenna, the hour-long film depicts the condition as a particular disposition rather than simply a disability. It features interviews with 9 top experts, and successful people living with the condition from all walks of life, while acknowledging "all the bad stuff as well," says Green.

"You'll be surprised at all the things we discovered," he says, somewhat mischievously. "The amount of misinformation out there is incredible. Even experts were surprised."

"One of the myths swiftly dispensed with is that meds are hugely dangerous or bad," he says. "Stimulant medications were first used to treat ADHD-type symptoms back in 1937! They are effective for 80 per cent of people who try them. For the remaining 20 per cent there is either no change or the benefits don't outweigh the side-effects, such as problems sleeping, weight loss, and so on. But everyone's experience is different."

"Teachers and parents report that kids with ADHD can flourish when they are on the right meds, especially when compared to the kids whose parents choose the drug-free route." Green's medication regime has included Ritalin, and later, Concerta. "Both are amazing and have made a big difference," he says. "What I got was that this helped turn down the constant background noise of thoughts. I once described it as the best cup of coffee in the world. And of course, caffeine is a stimulant as well."

But it was actually less than a decade ago when Green, 55, was diagnosed with the condition. Acceptance of the label was very much a Kubler-Ross (or grieving) process he says.

"At first, I was relieved at the diagnosis because I finally had an explanation for why I had so much on the go but nothing finished, poof listening skills, lost in thought, and more. Then I felt anger, then more anger after talking with friends and family who said the behaviour was associated with creativity. Then came regret and sadness as I lamented, 'had I but known.'"

Green likens ADHD to being on a dance floor with someone and grooving the night away on one leg that's about three inches shorter than the other and shifts to the left. Only what makes it such an insidious problem is that you have no idea that one leg is shorter than the other. You can't see ADHD.

"So there you are, out on the dance floor, trying to move like everyone else... and suddenly, you've knocked over your partner, and she's knocked over someone else, and they've knocked over the punch bowl, and suddenly you're left with this big mess all over the floor, and you're left feeling like a bad person. Worse, everyone is asking, 'What's wrong with you?!'"

You feel like an idiot. Or with ADHD, lazy, weak-willed, unreliable, stupid.

"It's a relief to realize you're not all those things. When someone points out that you have one leg longer than the other, suddenly a whole bunch of your life makes sense. This is why I was awful in gym class. This is why I walk in circles... Or whatever.

So, it's a relief to know. But then you're still out there on the dance floor and you start thinking about all the costs. All the ways it sabotaged you.

Eventually, I hope, you get past that. And then you wonder, 'Let's see what happens with a three-inch heel in my shoe."

And for the first time things are even, it levels the playing field... Or in this case, the dance floor. With ADHD, you're less chaotic, not losing things as much, and you're arriving on time. Which seems like a miracle."

Has ADHD helped his creativity at all? "It's helped me be trusting to allow ideas to flow," he says, reflecting on a long career that's included high water marks in Canadian television acting, writing, directing and producing stints on *The Red Green Show*, which ran for the better part of a decade.

Green's also known for creating, writing and acting in shows like TVO's *Prisoners of Gravity*, and *History Bites* for *History Television*. For several years he was a key player on CBC Radio's long-running *Frantic Times* featuring Toronto comedy troupe The Frantics. Along the way he wrote articles for *The Globe and Mail,* recorded comedy albums, acted in the odd movie, and received accolades and awards. Not bad for a youngster who started out as a teacher with the Ontario Science Centre.

"Creativity is a muscle that you build" he says. "One of the most satisfying things about being an artist is seeing something obvious nobody's ever noticed before. You are able to do something without being exploitive and show the truth as we know it."

That creativity and trademark humour is sure to be front and centre in the upcoming documentary, *ADD and Loving It?!*

"Of all the mental health diagnoses out there, this one is the most misunderstood, and brings so much hope," he says. "The brain is flexible and you can play to strengths and work around your weaknesses. If you can do that, you can soar."

In Person: Quinn Bradlee

The offspring of Washington royalty and literary lions Ben Bradlee and Sally Quinn, Quinn Bradlee offers hope and an online gathering place as the founder of LD social networking site Friends of Quinn.

When friends like actress/*View* co-host Whoopi Goldberg and director Steven Spielberg drop by to chat, you know you're on to something.

Indeed, these are just some of the guests who rub shoulders with Quinn Bradlee, founder of the influential Friends of Quinn (FOQ) website, which has become something of a cultural touchstone among people, young and old, in the LD community. Since its inception a few short years ago, FOQ has helped open up national dialogue among people living with learning differences, as Bradlee prefers to call LD, on topics like work, relationships and "fitting in."

Bradlee, 32, says the web site was originally conceived as a blog while he was working for a company called Health Central, but after that company folded the site was eventually taken over by the National Centre for Learning Disabilities. It's grown steadily ever since.

"One-eighth of Hollywood has dyslexia," he quips. "There's lots more than I thought!"

And while interviewees like Richard Branson and lawyer David Boice provide the star power, the site's real thrust is providing inspiration and dialogue, he says.

"When I think of a 'disability' I think of something that can't move," he says. "A vehicle can be disabled and won't move, for example. That's why I think of my situation as a learning difference. You learn differently, just at a different speed."

And Bradlee knows a thing or three about overcoming difficulties. Born with two holes in his heart that required invasive surgery when he was just three months old, Bradlee endured an apparently endless round of health challenges including seizures and migraines for most of his childhood. A diagnosis of velocardiofacial syndrome (VCFS) was finally made when Bradlee was 14. VCFS is little-known disorder affecting one-in-2000 people and manifests as a wide array of physical barriers and learning disabilities.

"VCFS is different for different people," says Bradlee. "In my case it's responsible for dyslexia and ADD. It's caused problems with reading comprehension and short-term memory in general."

To compensate, he's developed routines to aid in memory, something he might have learned while attending the Gow School, a college prep school for students with LD. He also attended the Lab School in Washington, DC, and the New York Film Academy.

The production skills he learned at the latter were channeled into an HBO film, *I Can't Do This, But I Can Do That*, a documentary about LD. He also co-authored two books, including *A Life's Work: Fathers and Sons,* a joint venture with his father.

For the uninitiated, his father just happened to be *Washington Post* editor Ben Bradlee, who was instrumental in publishing the Watergate stories that ultimately led to US President Richard Nixon's resignation. He passed away last year at 93. Bradlee *père's* third wife is no literary slouch or stranger to controversy herself: mama Sarah Quinn is also a best-selling author and journalist. As if that weren't enough, Bradlee's great uncle, Frank Crowinshield, left his mark on café society as the editor of a couple of rags called respectively, *Vogue* and *Vanity Fair.*

With credentials like that, publishing is literally in his blood. "I am a journalist, but I don't think of myself as that," he demurs. "I just collect stories and put them on my site."

As for the pressures that exist with living up to the famous family he was born into, he says, "people like Kim Kardashian are famous for being famous. I've learned that fame is really just being the right person in the right place at the right time and that's what makes you famous."

Fresh off an award granted by *Washington Life* magazine as one of the most influential people under 40 in their recent "Power and Personality" issue, Bradlee maintains a level-headed composure as he describes his mission in life.

"One of the reasons I'm creating this site is so that people don't have to be clichéd about learning differences," he says. I just want to show you'll have difficulties no matter your background, but you can still learn how to prosper."

The Fonz Goes to Windsor

Back in 2011 Henry Winkler published his first non-fiction book: a meditation on life refracted through the lens of a fly fisher. But this wasn't his literary endeavour. Over 19 others had preceded it! Not bad for the dyslexic offspring of parents that once christened him a "dumb dog." The fictional star of Winkler's kids' books is named Hank Zipzer. And it was never Fonzie who impressed me as much as Zipzer. The boy alter-ego in Winkler's mega-successful kids' book series, Zipzer, reflects many of the challenges that those of us with invisible disabilities face daily. Framed in warmth and humour, Winkler the child is Zipzer the adult. Along with roles in The Waterboy *and directing gigs, Winkler has truly proven that there's life after* Happy Days.*

We're in the basement of the Caboto Club in Windsor and Henry Winkler—best known and loved as Arthur "The Fonz" Fonzarelli from TV's *Happy Days*, and more recently for roles on TV's *Arrested Development* and for producing shows like *MacGyver* – is taking charge and clearly has a schedule to follow.

During the press conference, he waves all of us journalist types to the front, and advises he has enough time to answer at least two questions from each of us. He speaks rapidly, interrupts himself with joking asides, and clearly knows how to give "good quote."

But it may be a lesser-known fact that Winkler also has dyslexia. He's in town for a benefit for The Learning Disabilities Association of Windsor-

Essex, the agency headed by Executive Director Bev Clarke, who, along with her associates and sponsors, has done a smashing good job of organizing the event. Diagnosed with the learning disability at age 31, Winkler only learned of his own condition after his three children were all diagnosed with dyslexia themselves.

It's something he shares with the sold-out crowd later in the evening, after refreshing commentaries from Randolph Sealy and Joseph Casey, who have provided a good definition of learning disabilities. Winkler's main message, he tells the humming room, is that each child "has greatness in them. They need to figure out how to give to the world."

Acknowledging that growing up, he was "academically in the bottom three percent in North America," he developed a "high level of low self-esteem. My one word with which to live life would have to be 'tenacity.' My parents were Jews who fled Nazi Germany in 1939. I learned tenacity from them when what I needed was their pride."

The room nods in acknowledgement.

****

Right now, we're waiting for Winkler's arrival after being directed to the basement. There's a handful of journalists in the room, and we move around making polite introductions, nervously waiting. I meet a young woman completing a degree at Ryerson, another writer for *The Windsor Star*, still another from some television station.

Trying to arrange a telephone interview has been a downright pain. Bev Clarke has graciously provided the contact information for Winkler's agent, and a ridiculous electronic correspondence ping ponged back and forth for a couple of days. How long did I want to speak to him? When did I want to speak to him? What questions did I want answered?

I requested a half-hour, preferably after 5 p.m., Ontario time. "Mr. Winkler will give you 20 minutes, but does not give interviews after 2 p.m.,

California time," I was informed. Well then, I offered, attempting flexibility, I am sure I can accommodate his schedule. When would be good for him?"

An email arrives, declining the interview request. I write back suggesting it's unfair to lead me to believe an interview has been granted when it clearly hasn't. The agent apologizes for potentially misleading me, stating that Mr. Winkler is far too busy to grant interviews at the moment; he is on tour, and has a bronze bust unveiling to attend in Milwaukee. Headlines scream out the following day "Bronze the Fonz." Annoyed, I write Bev to tell her I'll be attending, and discover that Winkler will, in fact, talk to us, if only for a few minutes each during the press conference.

Suddenly he appears. It's hard to believe the guy who once epitomized cool is now 63. Despite a slight paunch—call him "The Paunz"--at five feet, six inches, he's shorter than expected, sports a shock of flowing grey locks, looks dapper in a sharp grey suit. He strides into the room smiling, making a point of shaking hands with everyone, and suddenly the nervous energy that permeated the room is gone. Everyone is at ease as Winkler talks with an infectious energy. He wastes no time making his point.

As a child, Winkler struggled with reading, writing, and math. "Everything but lunch," he cracks. Growing up, his parents' nickname for him was "dumb dog", a joke that quickly reached its best before date. "I learned to have a sense of humour. As an undiagnosed dyslexic, you spend a third of your time trying to figure out what's wrong with you, a third of your time trying to figure out why you can't figure it out, and the final third trying to cover up the shame and humiliation."

He states that living with dyslexia was cause for him to want to carve the condition "out of my brain with a spoon, but I realize now I might never have gotten where I am without it."

He struggled academically through high school, and had the negative message reinforced. He remembers one teacher telling him, he'd do well in life "if he ever graduated."

Rebelling against his parents' wishes to take over the family lumber business, he applied to 28 universities and was accepted into two. In 1967, he graduated with a Bachelor's degree from Emerson College before the defining moment came: applying to, and being accepted into Yale's drama program. "I stuck my head out the window and yelled that I got accepted into Yale," he fonz-ly recalls.

The "dumb dog" graduated with a master's degree in fine arts in 1970.

He started working almost immediately, doing television commercials during the day and theatre at night. In 1974, he won the part of a gang member in a Sylvester Stallone movie called *The Lords of Flatbush*, and shortly thereafter, auditioned for and won a small part in a little show called *Happy Days*, playing the part of high school dropout Arthur Fonzarelli.

The leather jacket, the motorcycle, the oft-imitated "Aaaaay," all became 1970s trademarks, and *Happy Days* ran for ten years becoming a cultural touchstone in the process. The 1970s were all about Fonzie, whose popularity grew along with his role. In 1984, after hanging the leather jacket up for good, he continued acting, but expanded his career to include producing and directing.

When I informed an editor friend, I was going to Windsor to meet Winkler, he showed his age by exclaiming, "You're going to go meet Barry Zuckerkorn?" Clearly, a new generation has grown up with Winkler, perhaps better known today for *Arrested Development* and movies like *Scream, Click* and *You Don't Mess With the Zohan*.

In recent years, he's also become a passionate advocate for children's welfare, working with numerous groups. He is involved with The MacLaren Children's Center (a facility for abused children), The National Committee for Arts for the Handicapped, The Special Olympics, and The Los Angeles Music Center's Very Special Arts Festival, as well as, numerous teenage alcohol and drug abuse programs. He is a founding member of the Children's Action Network, a non-profit organization that sponsors informational briefings for writers, producers and directors on children's concerns and serves as a clearinghouse for the entertainment industry on children's issues.

This guy with dyslexia has also discovered a new method of self-expression, expanding his resume to include something he thought he'd never become: a novelist. Now in touch with a completely new generation again, he, along with collaborator Lin Oliver, has authored 15 best-selling, award-winning children's books starring the autobiographical Hank Zipzer who, like Winkler, just happens to be a struggling student with a reading disability. With titles like *Barfing in the Backseat, The Life of Me*, and *The Curtain Went Up, My Pants Fell Down*, Winkler builds on his childhood experiences to chronicle a life familiar to many with dyslexia. In *The Life of Me*, Zipzer's print disability is accommodated by being allowed to present an autobiographical assignment in scrapbook form rather than an essay, and the book includes actual photographs and scrapbook snippets, something that many with dyslexia will be able to relate to.

When I ask how he accommodates himself in real life, Winkler stares blankly for a split second and says, "Well...I'm staying at Caesar's."

"No, no," I say, "I mean, how do you accommodate your disability?"

"Oh!" he snaps, and bounces right back, making a superb recovery. "I have an assistant who spells 'dessert' for me," he cracks. "You know, I only wrote my first email a year ago? And last week I discovered spell check! It's great!"

The room laughs, and soon Winkler is addressing a crowd of 1,200 adoring fans at the sold-out event upstairs. Slightly over an hour later, the hordes are lining the room, Zipzer books clutched firmly in hand, waiting for autographs and photo opportunities.

Sensing the slowness of the procession, Winkler jumps up and again takes control of the situation. "Look," he tells the crowd. "If we continue at this rate, you'll be waiting all weekend to have your books signed." He marches forward with a pen and starts moving along the wall, signing books, cracking jokes, posing for photographs, shaking hands. He's lifted the spirits of hundreds in attendance, communicated a positive message and maybe even given some hope.

Now that's pretty cool!

Hands Across the Water, Heads Across the Sky:
The Child Abuse Monument

Funny those rare and random acts that occasionally wind up having the most shockingly profound effect on you. Years after writing this piece, I still find myself shaking my head in disbelief at the accidental discovery of that strangely-shaped statue we happened upon in Toronto's Beaches neighbourhood following a mid-afternoon stroll along the nearby boardwalk. Strange that its creator was the curator of so much pain. Stranger still that the statue memorialized the life story of a man whose tragic ending outraged a nation, while generating attention on a subject many find difficult to discuss. In 2014, Queen's Park formally declined artist Michael Irving's magnificent artwork, which partially sits languishing, without a permanent display site, in the artist's basement. It's a painful contradiction to think that a piece of art, so potent and profound- -a gift to the world--remains homeless.

O n February 18, 1997, Martin Kruze stepped forward and told the world about his sexual abuse at the hands of former Maple Leaf Gardens employee, Gordon Stuckless.

The media ran with the story, coast-to-coast. For months it was difficult to avoid seeing or hearing how violation of young boys had occurred in the "temple of dreams" that was symbol of the great Canadian sport.

Reactions, of course, were mixed.

Some doubted the veracity of his story. Others became very uncomfortable with a subject that, to that point, received scant attention. Still others came forward to admit the same thing had happened to them. Whatever you felt about the story, Kruze was everywhere. After the media frenzy finally died down, Kruze went to work tirelessly volunteering, speaking, writing about sexual abuse and its devastating impact. But on October 30, 1997, three days after Stuckless was sentenced to two years less-a-day for violating 24 boys, Kruze committed suicide.

According to a 2007 Statistics Canada report, 53,400 children and youth were victims of a police-reported assault the previous year. The risk of abuse, of course, is thought to be at least five times greater for people with disabilities than the rest of the population, and most victims are violated by someone they know. According to the Disabled Women's Network of Ontario, up to 90% of all women with disabilities will suffer from abuse at some point in their lifetime. Furthermore, people with disabilities are more likely targets of sexual abuse because the ability to communicate their violation is more difficult due to speech issues, isolation or credibility. The reality is disquieting.

****

A few days after Martin Kruze's death, Dr. Michael Irving was approached by the Kruze family. Irving, a psychotherapist and artist, creator of The Child Abuse monument, had spoken with Kruze about participating in the project, and now, in death, Kruze was still making a contribution to promoting knowledge about sexual abuse. With a cast of Kruze's hand and the words, "Martin's Hope" engraved on a patch of bronze quilt that forms the core of the statue, he is remembered. Hauntingly, an image of Kruze at the age when his abuse occurred rests just below the cast of his hand.

Indeed, the monument is hard to miss. Directly inspired by The Vietnam Monument, the sculpture, properly entitled, Reaching Out, is actually two figures together measuring 11-foot high and 30-feet wide. The figures stand imposingly, arms reaching out and skyward, forming an arch wide enough for three people to walk through. Embedded within the figures are a series of quilts (or squares) created by survivors of abuse and their supporters. Each square is unique: some are quite simple, others more complex. All are poignant. Here, a hand reaches out to a bird on a branch, possibly a hawk. There, a hand either rises out of or sinks into a pool of water. The viewer is left to decide. In yet another square, a child's tiny hand sits below the hands of his parents, with the words, "May hope be passed through every hand" floating beside.

It's not all doom and gloom. Some squares carry visceral, empowering messages, including a hand that hovers open on its square, a mouth between the thumb and index finger, with the words, "I will be heard" scattered around. In yet another, a human embryo rests content in the palm of a hand with guardians, including a rabbit, lion and dog surrounding it. Others represent aboriginal forms of healing.

Additionally, there are 22 plain quilt squares, left blank intentionally so all survivors of sexual abuse can be remembered. Alternatively, visitors can dampen their hands in the fountain that fronts the memorial and leave their own wet, temporary hand print on the statue as a way of being indirectly involved with the work.

It should come as no surprise that some of these hand prints featured in the work are those belonging to people with learning disabilities. But it may be a bit more surprising to learn that the Monument's artist was diagnosed with LDs himself.

"At 34, I had the writing level of a fifth-or-sixth grader," he says. "I believe the impact of the abuse made my learning disabilities unable to be coped with."

Irving grew up in a home he describes as "violent and abusive." Out of 12 children, he states seven were illegitimate. At his father's funeral, several friends described his father as the angriest person they had ever known.

Early on, he turned to art, recognizing its healing properties. He became interested in sculpture and painting. Further healing came later by exploring his First Nations roots. Through his own healing work, he developed not only a richer sense of self, but also the ability to have compassion for others.

"Acts of compassion are the most rewarding things that a person can do and being able to be compassionate gives the greatest meaning. It can almost be viewed as selfish in terms of what comes back."

Much of that compassion goes into the psychotherapy practice he runs in Toronto's east end.

"I get a sense of being a teacher and sharing skills to manage a life," he says. Hopefully they'll (clients) impart some of that. I have a sense of a rippling effect because of their time spent with me."

When working with trauma survivors, Irving's style is to always look for what is fundamentally positive about the person. He recognizes that behaviours and symptoms that are presented are not always what is implied.

"With trauma survivors, their symptoms are often the best response they could make at the time to a horrible situation," he says. "Therefore what may be seen as a disability, or disabling, may have its roots in being an ability. So, I always look for assets and strengths. "

The same applies to his own learning disability. "At the core of dyslexia, there's a sense of freedom of thought about what is truth," he says. "I'm not confined to the structure of language in the same way I don't feel confined to the structure of social beliefs."

Those social beliefs often dictate that sexual abuse should not be discussed. Typically, Irving went against the grain to attain his vision and honour his commitment to seeing the project through to its completion.

Over a painstaking number of years, through dozens of public consultations and focus groups, workshops on sexual abuse, and unending rounds of funding applications, the project gradually began to take shape. Eventually, he amassed over 1,000 pages of documentation as the project was being conceived. Irving consulted abuse survivors, artists, psychologists before identifying three characteristics the Monument had to possess, says Irving.

"It needed to be personal, collaborative and include storytelling," says Irving. "I came up with the idea of a hand print of it being personal and borrowed from female artists when I decided to use a quilt for collaboration."

But it's the stories woven into the bronze quilt that are the most riveting aspects of the sculpture. Names are named; angry, sad, empowering stories are reported.

Yoko Ono once famously remarked that "art was a verb" meaning that her work was an invitation to be interactive with the viewer, rather than the viewer being a passive recipient of the work. The Monument functions much the same way.

Irving states the piece is a good example of "projective identification," meaning that the viewer can engage with it. "We all have had the experience of seeing a movie and coming out feeling changed." says Irving.

"Consciously or not, previous conflicts have been massaged and you have changed in the darkness of the theatre. The Monument is a piece of art in which a survivor can engage in this process of projective identification.

"A few hundred survivors put heart and soul into these art works," he says. "They did so because they knew the Monument would be around for centuries and would have a positive impact on generations of people who were coping with an adversity they themselves had been through."

By visiting the Monument website you can cast your vote of support to have the Provincial government accept the donation of the finished Bronze Monument to Queen's Park, and you can also find out how you can have you own handprint message permanently placed inside one of the Monument figures.

Coach's Corner

I was indeed privileged to know and work with the late and lovely Barbara Durst, one of Canada's first ADHD coaches. Her steady, stable presence and calm centeredness guided many individuals through the boiling storm-sea of ADHD diagnosis to the shores of self-discovery. While cancer claimed her life far too early, her legacy lives on in a generation of coaches who have since followed, and the legion of people who have managed to come home to themselves after she so profoundly touched their lives.

W hen Jim Darley, a computer consultant in Mississauga, ON, feels the going getting tough, he has a simple solution: he reaches across his desk and hits the big red "easy" button.

The five-dollar item, purchased at an office supply store, utters a pre-recorded voice stating, "That was easy!" and for a time, the world feels a little less heavy.

That's because the soft-spoken Darley, 58, who was only diagnosed with Attention Deficit Disorder (ADD) in September after decades of self-doubt and repeated failures, is still adjusting to his new label. The button serves as a kind of self-regulating "check-in" tool that helps keep him focused. "It may sound silly, but the button reminds me to ask myself, 'Are you still doing what you meant to be doing?'" says Darley.

Purchasing the button was a suggestion from Darley's ADHD coach, Barbara Durst, who has been in the business of providing support services for adults with ADHD for over a decade. (The "H" stands for "hyperactivity," which affects many people with this disorder.) She emphasizes that coaching is a holistic process. "You have to start coaching the human, the person," says Durst. "Coaching is about changing thoughts to behaviour, and you're helping a person actualize their dreams while guiding them in managing their lives and the real world around them."

ADHD coaching is a form of client-driven lifestyle coaching that is structured around the recipient's unique needs. Believed to have been developed over a decade ago by American Madelyn Griffith- Haynie of The Optimal Functioning Institute in Tennessee, coaching can be adapted to the neurological wiring and behaviours that create barriers for the person living with ADHD in work, school and life. Durst emphasizes that coaching uses a pragmatic, outcome-based approach to achieve realistic goals.

Once thought to be the "disorder du jour," ADHD is now accepted as a legitimate neurological disability that affects about four percent of the population. It's a disability in which the brain's frontal lobes — responsible for targeting, integrating and synthesizing data from other parts of the brain and filtering out distractions — malfunction, letting in all kinds of visual and auditory distractions, overloading the brain. Depending on the individual, the brain can either become over- or under-stimulated. This can result in a wide range of responses, from feeling overwhelmed to disengaging from situations.

It is generally agreed that there are three types of ADHD: Impulsive, often characterized by a short attention span and hyperactivity; Inattentive, which tends to manifest itself as daydreaming, procrastination and a tendency to leave complex tasks unfinished, and a combination of the two. ADHD frequently co-exists with other disorders, including learning disabilities, anxiety and depression. ADHD is not an intellectual disability — people with this disability often have average or above-average intelligence.

ADHD at Work

In the workplace, where skills such as planning, teamwork and organization are seen as critical to a company's success, employees with ADHD often falter. Problems with auditory processing and short-term memory, which affect many people with ADHD, only complicate the situation further. Because ADHD is an "invisible" disability, many workers remain undiagnosed. People with ADHD may also be unemployed or under-employed because employers don't understand the condition.

In some cases, ADHD symptoms lead to years of frustration. "When I was finally diagnosed, everything fell into place," says Darley. "I had an inability to stay on topic, and lots of great ideas — a constant flow — but lots of incomplete projects."

Typically, ADHD coaching begins with a consultation, where the coach collects data about the client's experiences and challenges. The coach inquires about goals and changes the client wants to make before settling on frequency of contact, duration of meetings and fees. "I ask what changes they want to make in their lives; there's usually a defining reason why they want a coach," says Durst.

The right "fit" between a coach and client is probably the most important element in a successful coaching relationship, says Toronto ADHD coach, LouAnne Babcook, who is working toward certification through The Optimal Functioning Institute. "Otherwise the relationship won't be as productive or rewarding as it could be."

The issues clients bring to the table can include time management, financial management, relationships, decision-making or just getting things done. "There's an emphasis on the practical, and a lot of time is spent with the coach trying to glean information and identify issues," says Babcook. "You gain insights when things don't go well, and you hear a lot of negative self-talk. We need to work on rewriting that script."

Getting Organized

Perhaps the most consistent issue that clients seek assistance for is disorganization. It's a problem that often comes down to executive functioning — logic and problem-solving — says Durst. "The person's wiring doesn't allow him or her to access processing to help with planning or organization, and they get overwhelmed. Being able to choose between what's important and what's interesting and knowing those choices will help them move forward in positive ways."

Many clients take advantage of inexpensive items like alarm clocks, day planners, sticky notes, calendars and Blackberries to help manage their ADHD. These are what Durst calls "triggers" that help ritualize actions and convert negatives, such as chronic lateness, into positive, consistent behaviours. Other simple techniques include decluttering workspaces and setting simple, manageable deadlines, which may also include taking lots of breaks in between.

"I've been made more conscious of when I'm getting off track and have learned to pause when this happens," says Darley, who started working with Durst last summer when he suspected he had ADD. (It was Durst who suggested he seek an official diagnosis from a doctor.)

The other ingredients that make coaching work are consistency, positive reinforcement and a proper balance of medications, such as Adderall, Ritalin or Strattera. Over time, clients learn to articulate their concerns and become effective self-advocates. It can be a lengthy process, taking up to six months, with the client and coach meeting at least once a week until the client develops self-management skills. It can also be costly, with some clients paying up to $500 monthly.

Finding a Coach

ADHD coaching is not yet as prevalent in Canada as it is in the United States, but the field is growing. When considering working with a coach, it's best to look for someone with special training and credentials in working with clients who have ADHD. The Optimal Functioning Institute was the first to certify ADHD coaches, and there are now others, as well. Durst, for example, graduated from Coach U, has obtained a Master Coaching designation from The Optimal Functioning Institute, and is also certified as a professional certified coach by the International Coach Federation.

You should carefully screen potential coaches to gain an understanding of how much they know about ADHD. Find out if they're certified and by whom. Also consider whether you and the coach have a good "fit" — do you feel comfortable sharing details of your life with the person? What techniques does he or she use? Might an ADHD support group also be helpful to you?

"The whole point of coaching is just to make things easier," says Darley. He still considers himself a "work in progress," but his stress management and coping mechanisms have already improved with coaching. "Coaching helps to build self-esteem and the process is very genuine. It's nice to have someone reminding you of your strengths and offering something positive."

Seeking Sanctuary:
Finding Sacred Places Afar and Close to Home

When Ken Seaton finally reached the top of that pyramid in Teotihuacan, Mexico, something strange happened — he felt at peace. Despite the chronic and acute back pain that Seaton had experienced ever since a workplace accident caused mobility problems years earlier, he made the arduous 30-minute climb up the uneven steps and, for the first time in years, realized that he felt no pain.

"It was mind-blowing," Seaton says excitedly, recalling the day he made the journey to the pyramid 60 kilometres northeast of Mexico City. "I almost felt lifted by unseen forces. I wasn't tired or in pain, and I experienced such a sense of wellness, I can't even begin to describe it." He adds that Teotihuacan is known as the place "where man becomes God," a belief that evolved out of local and ancient Toltec mythology.

Seaton is one of countless people who journey to sacred and symbolic places around the world in search of peace, answers to profound questions or a connection to a power greater than themselves. For millennia, pilgrims of all faiths and cultures have journeyed to sacred sites and places of worship, such as Jerusalem's Wailing Wall, the pyramids of Egypt, Mecca in Saudi Arabia or Stonehenge in England, often travelling thousands of kilometres. The lure of these scattered places is the belief that they hold spiritual power or energy, and that visitors can be transformed or healed by it. The outward journey to a sacred place mirrors the inward journey to the divine.

Sacred architecture can be a link between the earth and the spirit, providing a focus for nurturing the soul and healing the self. In a world that seems to move faster and get more complicated every day, these sanctuaries offer opportunities for respite, resolution and reflection.

Road to Spiritual Riches

Spiritual yearning drove Chrystalla Chew to make an 800-kilometre pilgrimage to Spain. Chew, who lives with learning disabilities, is a soft-spoken former recruiter who left the corporate world a decade ago to pursue a more spiritual existence. In 2000, she followed the route famously known as El Camino, which is said to trace the path of The Milky Way and reflect the energy of the stars above it. She walked from the Pyrenees in France to Santiago de Compostela in the western reaches of Galicia Spain, a journey that took 41 days.

El Camino has attracted pilgrims from all over the world, many of whom are not affiliated with any particular religion, but seek a spiritual connection all the same. It is believed that after the death of Christ, his disciples scattered throughout the globe to spread the gospel. James is said to have gone to Spain, later returning to Jerusalem, where he was beheaded by Herod. His body was returned to Spain and entombed in a hillside near Santiago de Compostela, where he rested for 750 years. In the ninth century, a hermit had a vision of a unique star arrangement over a deserted spot in the hills. James' remains were rediscovered, and King Alfonso II declared him the patron saint of Spain. A church was built over the tomb in

James' honour. A town grew around the church, and it became a pilgrimage centre.

At the height of El Camino's popularity in the eleventh century, over half a million pilgrims are said to have completed the journey. In recent years the pilgrimage has made a comeback, bolstered by among other things, the 1989 visit of Pope John Paul II and actress Shirley MacLaine's book about her pilgrimage in the mid-1990s.

Chew's journey gave her a chance to reflect on her place in the world. "I felt a sense of real humility knowing so many had stood where I was standing: The Pope, St. Francis of Assisi...I felt my greatness and smallness and connection to humanity. So many had walked before me. I was such a small dot in the great scheme of things; I felt such gratitude," says Chew, who is also a reiki master and co-founder of The Amethyst Reiki Centre in Campbellford, ON. The experience was so fulfilling that, at press time, Chew had embarked on another pilgrimage, one that will take her through China, Japan, Singapore and Thailand.

Toronto resident Manjusri Welikala, who has been blind since age 14, was deeply moved by his pilgrimage to the temple Kataragama in his native Sri Lanka. The temple is visited by thousands of Buddhists, Hindus and Muslims annually.

"The temple is the residence of the six-faced Skanda, supreme commander of the gods and epitome of knowledge," says Welikala. He had visited the temple many times, but says it became more meaningful after he became blind. "It's different when you're blind. For me, I have to have the feeling of something bigger or better than what we see. Because of my disability, this takes on added significance. Vision for me is sound. Even in meditation, there is a mantra repeated over in my mind. The vibrations of the place need to feel good." Welikala, who has also undertaken journeys to sites in the United States and Canada, enjoys hearing the stories and history of each place he visits, as they create context for his own experiences.

Barriers on the Path

Accessibility can be a problem at ancient sites. "Most temples have steps that make it difficult for people using wheelchairs," says Welikala. "Temples don't go the extra mile to welcome people with disabilities. I feel that Eastern places are not all that willing to accommodate, either. They expect you to bring someone with you. In Canada, though, I find they are more accommodating."

Many places of worship offer outdoor pathways called labyrinths, which are accessible. Intended for meditation, the patterns of many labyrinths are modelled on spirals from nature, and their designs date back as far as 4,000 years. Many cultures have labyrinth-like symbols. In First Nations communities, it is called the Medicine Wheel. The Celts call it The Never Ending Circle. Mystical Judaism refers to it as the Kabbalah. One of the most famous is within the cathedral in Chartres, France.

Labyrinths can be used to calm the mind and find balance. They are open to all people as an accessible, non-denominational tool of the spirit and can be found in medical centres, parks, churches, schools, prisons and even in people's backyards.

Labyrinths are not mazes. They follow a single path that winds to the centre. Once you reach it, you turn around and go back. The path, in full view, allows a participant to focus internally. There are many ways to approach a labyrinth, but it is often viewed in three stages: releasing tension and worry on the way in, being receptive and meditative in the centre, and returning to the world with new insight.

Homing Instinct

Since accessing ancient sites can be difficult and costly, it's important to find or create sacred places closer to home. In doing so, we establish a place to nurture the soul, honour ourselves and create a place for renewal and ritual. This is especially necessary if access to sites in the outside world is limited, challenging and frustrating.

As many people do, Chrystalla Chew once believed that only churches or nature could offer spiritual experiences. Now, she knows that you don't have to travel far or spend a lot of money to find meaningful places. "A sacred space can be anywhere," says Chew. She adds that even the busy corner of Yonge and Dundas Streets in Toronto's downtown core can be a sacred space. "It is where we take our attitude and vibration that brings that sacredness out."

Ken Seaton and Manjusri Welikala enjoy travelling, but they also cultivate private sanctuaries in their own homes. Seaton has a special chair that keeps him centred, and he has scattered crystals throughout his apartment for their positive energy. And, although Welikala can't see his surroundings, he takes great care to create an aesthetically pleasing space. "Where you live has to be sacred. I associate where I live as a part of me, so I keep it clean, take off my shoes. I fill my space with pictures, plants, convenience."

When planning your own space, keep it simple. You can create an altar in any room of your home and fill it with simple, meaningful things, such as family photos, feathers, stones, candles, beads and plants. Include religious items if they hold meaning for you. All of these objects invite and celebrate the spiritual part of ourselves. They also provide focus and stimulate sensations and memories. A water-smoothed stone once found on a beach can instantly bring back a connection with nature, for example. Once established, sensorial facilitators like music and burning incense can intensify the experience.

You can also create your space outdoors, in your garden or backyard. Fill it with flowers and herbs that have relaxing, soothing scents. Try meditation or yoga. Experiment with the Chinese art of feng shui or its Indian counterpart, Vaastu. Both of these philosophies aim to increase harmony in living spaces by strategically arranging objects or designing architecture to improve the flow of energy (chi in Chinese and prana in Sanskrit). These arts have become popular in North America in recent years – corporations even hire feng shui experts to optimize the energy flow in their offices.

What's most important about creating your sacred space, however, is the intent behind it. Do you wish the space to be a respite from a harsh, external world? A place to meditate, breathe and reconnect with yourself and your body? A place to worship a deity? There is no single "right" way to cultivate and use a sacred space. Knowledge of rituals is helpful, but not essential. The most important thing is what it means to you.

Sacred spaces are a reflection of desire to live life more mindfully, to explore things and ideas that we find meaningful, and honour our place in the world. The geography of that place is vast, of course, because the ultimate journey we embark on is the one that starts within.

Carter Hammett is a social worker, writer and trainer who spent his childhood between Ottawa and Prince Albert SK. He graduated from Cape Breton University with a Bachelor of Community Studies degree and holds diplomas in social work, adult education and journalism. His words and pictures have appeared in *The Toronto Sun, The National Post, The Toronto Star, The Ottawa Citizen, Abilities Magazine, Convenience and Carwash Canada* and *Auto and Trucking Atlantic*. He is the author of two previous books, including the well-received *Benchmarking: A Guide to Hiring and Managing Persons with Learning Disabilities* (ALDER, 2005). He currently lives in Toronto. Visit his website at www.wordgarden.ca

www.ingramcontent.com/pod-product-compliance
Lightning Source LLC
Chambersburg PA
CBHW062103270326
41931CB00013B/3195